Original title:
Christmas Eve by Candlelight

Copyright © 2024 Creative Arts Management OÜ
All rights reserved.

Author: Jasper Montgomery
ISBN HARDBACK: 978-9916-90-930-0
ISBN PAPERBACK: 978-9916-90-931-7

Moments Woven in Golden Light

In the morning's gentle sway,
Cats plot mischief in bright sunray.
Coffee spills, oops, what a sight,
Laughter dances, hearts feel light.

Childhood tales of ghosts and fright,
Are just socks that took to flight.
Granny's yarn, a tangled delight,
We craft our dreams, oh what a height!

The Echo of Candles in the Night

With candles flickering, shadows play,
I saw a ghost, or was it clay?
A late-night snack, oh what a fright,
The fridge just whispered, 'Come, take a bite!'

Friends gathered 'round, jokes take flight,
One lost a marshmallow to the light.
Stories spun, the laughter bright,
The echoes dance, oh what a night!

Luminous Strings of Harmony

We strum the tunes, off-key delight,
A cat meows, here comes the fright.
Our voices clash, a funny plight,
Yet still the stars twinkle so bright.

In the garden, a talent show,
The veggies cheer, they steal the glow.
A carrot sings, the onions flow,
We laugh till dawn, the night's tableau!

The Quiet Magic of Gathering

Around the table, tales unfold,
Of burnt casseroles, all too bold.
A dog steals dinner, oh behold,
In the chaos, warmth takes hold.

Laughter rises, spirits lift,
With silly games, we share the gift.
Family bonds, a gentle rift,
In every moment, love's soft shift.

Echoes of Luminance

In a room full of laughter,
A toaster found some bread,
It popped up like a champion,
Said, 'What's for breakfast ahead?'

The cat looked quite suspicious,
With eyes like shiny disks,
It plotted how to eat that toast,
While everyone just risks.

The fridge hummed a soft beat,
Swaying with its cool tune,
While the spoons danced with forks,
In a metal festival at noon.

Then came the coffee jug,
Saying, 'Let's brew some cheer!'
But tripped on a peanut shell,
And gave us all a scare!

Warm Wishes in the Twilight

As stars begin to twinkle,
The moon put on its hat,
It stepped out for a stroll,
With a dancing acrobat.

The breeze carried whispers,
Of dreams from afar,
A squirrel with a skateboard,
Zoomed past a wishing star.

Candles flickered loudly,
With a flick of their flame,
They whispered warm emotions,
As if they knew our name.

So here's a cozy moment,
In the twilight's soft embrace,
Warm wishes in the night,
As we all find our place.

Festive Glow in the Heart

In the kitchen there's chaos,
With cookies on the floor,
Flour flying like confetti,
Who knew baking could be a chore?

The dog wears a Santa hat,
But he thinks it's just a snack,
He barks at the jingle bells,
And gives the whole bag a whack.

Candles lined the table,
On a tablecloth of cheer,
But one stubborn reindeer,
Is now glued to a beer.

Laughter fills the air now,
With stories fun to share,
In the glow of festive lights,
We spread good vibes everywhere!

Shadows that Hold Our Stories

In twilight's gentle embrace,
Shadows begin to play,
They whisper tiny secrets,
Of the silly things we say.

Like when Uncle Joe tripped,
While searching for a sock,
The stories that we treasure,
Are hidden in the clock.

There's a tale of the cat,
Who thought he ruled the house,
Till the dog found his throne,
And made him flee like a mouse.

So let's gather these shadows,
In a hug of twilight glow,
For each tale that they carry,
Is a treasure we all know.

Hope's Flame in the Quiet Night

In the stillness of the dark,
A candle flickers with a spark,
It whispers tales of dreams so bright,
Making shadows dance with delight.

Each flicker brings a joyful grin,
A secret wish for what's within,
For even when the world feels tight,
Hope's flame shines on through the night.

The Art of Candlelight Conversations

Gather 'round with friends so dear,
The wax drips down, but we don't fear,
With laughter rising, words take flight,
In the glow of soft candlelight.

We share our dreams and funny tales,
Of clumsy moments and silly fails,
In the warm flicker, hearts feel bright,
These chats make everything feel right.

Shadows Merged with Soft Radiance

Shadows waltz in candle's glow,
A hide-and-seek, a cosmic show,
They twist and turn, with grace they flow,
Creating scenes we never know.

Laughter mingles with each beam,
Life's just better than it seems,
For in the softness of the night,
Shadows dance with pure delight.

Hearts Alight in Gentle Twilight

As twilight wraps the day in gold,
We gather 'round, our stories told,
With hearts aglow and smiles wide,
In this warmth, we all confide.

A toast to mishaps and sweet puns,
As the day ends and the moon runs,
In gentle light, we find our might,
Hearts alight, everything feels right.

Secrets Illuminated by Wax

In the dark, secrets flicker bright,
Wax spills stories, what a sight!
Melted whispers, gooey delight,
Tonight's the night, we'll take flight.

Candles dance with a playful grin,
Tales of love, and where we've been.
Each little flame, a tiny win,
Laughter fades, but memories spin.

Some say wax can melt the tears,
But it can't help with your weird fears!
As shadows play, we shed our gears,
With every flicker, we toast our beers!

So lift your glass to the glowing light,
To secrets shared in the velvety night.
With friends beside and spirits bright,
We revel in wax, what pure delight!

The Calm of Candlelit Souls

In a room lit soft by flick'ring flames,
We ponder life and all its games.
Candlelight whispers, calling names,
While shadows play their silly claims.

Sipping tea that's gone all cold,
As we swap tales, nervous and bold.
Wax drips down where stories unfold,
Making faces, we laugh uncontrolled.

Each glow reveals a secret spree,
Of quirky wishes, and wild glee.
Among the flickers, we find our key,
Unlocking laughter, you and me.

So let's bask in this waxy peace,
Where worries vanish and troubles cease.
In candlelight, our hearts increase,
To silly dreams that never fleece!

Gathering by the Radiant Glow

Gather 'round the candle's gleam,
Where every flicker fuels a dream.
With cheeky jokes, we plot and scheme,
Creating chaos, like a team!

The waxy warriors stand so tall,
With melting courage, we'll never fall.
In this glow, we have a ball,
With laughter ringing, it's a hall!

As shadows laugh and tales unfurl,
A dance of mischief starts to swirl.
Beneath the light, the crazies twirl,
In candlelight, friendships pearl!

So grab a seat, it's time to show,
How with each glow, our spirits grow.
In this gathering, we'll steal the show,
By the radiant glow, we all bestow!

Radiant Whispers of Hope

Hope's a funny little ghost,
Hiding in your morning toast.
With a wink, it dares to dance,
And offers life's peculiar chance.

It sings beneath the kitchen sink,
In socks that vanish—what do you think?
It tickles hearts with silly glee,
And whispers jokes—just wait and see.

When clouds roll in, it wears a grin,
And turns your frown to silly kin.
Hope's a jester, quirky, spry,
It might just make your troubles fly!

So raise a cup to whims that float,
To jiving hope that loves to gloat!
In every giggle, every joke,
Sail through life—just be the bloke!

Mistletoe and Mystique

Under mistletoe's cheeky spell,
Kisses fly like elves from hell.
With each peck, a giggle grows,
As awkward as a dancing nose!

The holiday lights twinkle around,
While cats chase bows—what a sound!
Cookies cluelessly burn with glee,
As we laugh 'til we can't see!

Penguins in sweaters strut the floor,
Old tales of 'who opened the door?'
Decorations fall, then rise like art,
Mystique in chaos—it's all from the heart!

So grab a treat, raise your glass,
In this grand melee, let giggles amass.
Mistletoe leaves us with one clear beat:
The fun we share makes life so sweet!

Candlelit Revelations

In glow of wax, secrets flow,
Like revelations on the go.
The shadows dance, the flames can't wait,
For laughter draws them out—how great!

Each flicker tells a tale so bright,
Of spoons that tried to take their flight.
Candlelight giggles behind closed doors,
Cooking mishaps and sticky floors.

Revelations rise like fluffy bread,
Surprises wait 'til we're in bed.
The fridge makes noises, does it sigh?
Or just the leftovers—oh, my, oh my!

So light a flame, embrace the quirk,
As cozy smiles begin to work.
In every crackle, let spills be told,
Candlelit secrets, purest gold!

Serenity in Soft Light

In the soft light where dreams collide,
A funny thought starts to abide.
"Why did the pillow join the band?"
"Because it knew how to make a stand!"

In twilight's calm, ideas bloom,
Dreams jiggle around the room.
The socks debate who's the worst pair,
While dust bunnies float through the air.

Serenity sings a lullaby,
As mismatched chairs begin to fly.
Every giggle's a gentle breeze,
Tickling thoughts like rustling leaves.

So dim the light, but lift your heart,
Embrace the whimsy, play your part.
In softest glimmers, let worries pass,
Serenity's here—rise up and laugh!

The Poetry of Flickering Light

In the corner a bulb starts to dance,
Its flicker a funny little prance.
It winks and it blinks, oh what a sight,
Making shadows laugh in the warm twilight.

The lamp seems to have a secret to tell,
With each wobble, it casts a spell.
I wonder if it dreams of the sun,
Or perhaps it's plotting to finally run.

When dinner is served, it doesn't sit still,
Spinning stories while giving a thrill.
Oh, flickering light, you champion of cheer,
We're all quite convinced you're sipping cold beer!

And when the power goes out, oh the strife!
We miss your bright jokes loitering in life.
But fear not, dear light, we always will write,
About your wild tales under the night.

Chants Beneath the Stars

Look up at the sky, it's a cosmic show,
Stars are twinkling a whimsical glow.
They hum a tune that tickles the soul,
While we dance below, feeling quite whole.

Comets zoom by, with a wink and a grin,
Leaving trails behind, round and round we spin.
Moonbeams giggle, they play hide and seek,
While owls throw parties—how cheeky and sweet!

Sing to the night, let the laughter arise,
We're all stargazers, no need for disguise.
Under this blanket of cosmic delight,
Let's shout our joy to the magical night!

So raise up your voices, let's chant in glee,
The stars are our friends, come join in the spree.
With every bright twinkle and chuckle above,
We dance 'neath the stars, surrounded by love.

Nighttime Echoes of Warmth

As darkness descends, the echoes resound,
A symphony of laughter, all around.
Cozy and snug, with blankets galore,
We giggle and snort till we can't take more.

The kettle whistles, like it's lost its mind,
Spilling boiling secrets, so intertwined.
Cookies are crumbling, a sweet little mess,
While bedtime approaches, we're far from rest!

Whispers of stories float through the air,
The shadows collect, as if they could care.
Each creak of the floor is a slapstick sound,
Carrying joy that's delightfully profound.

So here's to the night, with its warmth and its cheer,
Where laughter is endless, and everyone's near.
Let's cherish the echoes, and hold them so tight,
As we snuggle and snack, 'neath the stars tonight.

Shadows with a Touch of Magic

Shadows creeping, oh what a sight,
Dancing on walls, taking flight.
They tiptoe along as if they were shy,
With a flick of the wrist, they whirl and they fly.

Oh, the ghost of a cat with a swishing tail,
Whispers soft secrets, we giggle and pale.
A shadow magician, casting delight,
Turning all darkness into pure light!

With blanket forts built to conquer the gloom,
Our shadows take charge, lighting up the room.
They juggle our fears and tickle our laughs,
Making us heroes of our own silly drafts.

So let's raise a toast to these magical friends,
Their charm and their tricks, it never quite ends.
In the light of the moon, we know it's true,
Shadows with magic are just made for you!

Serenity in a Time of Wonder

In the midst of chaos, I find my peace,
A cat on my lap, my worries release.
The world spins around, a carnival ride,
But here in my haven, I happily hide.

Emails and meetings, they come and they go,
I'll play hide and seek with my fuzzy burrito.
With snacks in my hand, I watch the time pass,
Who knew simple moments could feel like a blast?

The neighbor is mowing, a squeaky old machine,
Which makes my retreat feel like a dream so serene.
I lift up my voice to indulge in a song,
And suddenly feel that the day can't go wrong.

So here's to the chaos that swirls all about,
With a laugh and a grin, I'll ride every doubt.
In a time full of wonder, I choose to delight,
With silliness serving as my guiding light.

Dancing Flames of Togetherness

At the campfire's edge, we roast marshmallows,
As the flames dance lively, chasing away shadows.
With friends all around, we share silly tales,
Like the time that Bob tripped on his own flails.

The crackle and pop, a musical treat,
While laughter erupts with each sugary feat.
We argue and jest about who's the best,
At making the s'mores—it's a sugary test.

The stars peek down, watching us play,
While we howl like wolves in a playful way.
Around the warm fire, we lose track of time,
With stories and giggles, life feels so sublime.

Embers a-glow in the chilly night air,
Our hearts are aglow with the love that we share.
In the warmth of the flames, the world's troubles fade,
As we dance with each other, together, unafraid.

Nightfall's Blanket of Light

As the sun bids goodbye with a colorful glow,
The stars start to twinkle, putting on quite a show.
The moon in its glory, a beacon so bright,
Hangs like a lamp in the velvet of night.

The critters come out for their evening parade,
While I sneak to the fridge for a snack that I've made.
With cookies in hand, I sit down to stare,
At the wonders above, as if no one would care.

My neighbors, they think that I'm missing the fun,
Yet I'm in a world where my dreams can outrun.
For each twinkling star is a wish in disguise,
And I make them all boldly, under dark skies.

So here in the night, when the world's gone to rest,
I'll count my sweet blessings and feel so blessed.
The chaos can wait, let it trail far behind,
As I bask in this beauty, unique and one of a kind.

Soft Glows of Festive Cheer

With twinkling fairy lights strung all around,
The season of laughter and joy does abound.
Cookies are baking, the scent fills the air,
It's a sprightly reminder to jump in with flair.

As the carols ring out, I can't help but dance,
In pajamas and socks, I give it a chance.
My dog shakes his head, quite baffled by me,
But he joins in the fun, that's how it should be!

With family gathered, we share silly glee,
And swap outlandish gifts, just wait, you'll see!
A sweater from Grandma with reindeer that glows,
Or socks with flamingos, now that's how it goes!

So let's raise a toast to this whimsical time,
Where laughter and joy make our hearts feel like prime.
In this season of cheer, may we all lend an ear,
To the soft glowing magic that brings us all near.

The Light of Togetherness and Cheer

In a room filled with laughter and pie,
We dance like penguins, oh my, oh my!
With friends all around, we sing out loud,
And wear silly hats, looking quite proud.

The snacks are a treasure, the drinks overflow,
Someone brought pickles—what a strange show!
With clashing of voices and jokes that we share,
We brighten the night, like stars in the air.

The cat makes a leap and lands in the dip,
While Uncle Joe gives a very strange tip.
"Just add a bit of this, and a dash of that,"—
Oh, Uncle Joe, you're a culinary brat!

Here's to the moments, like balloon animals,
That shape our hearts and break the dull panels.
In the glow of togetherness, we do declare,
These nights filled with joy, oh, we really care!

Reflections of the Past in Gentle Glow.

I stumbled on photos from years gone by,
With hairstyles so wild, they made me cry.
In neon leotards, we danced like a fool,
Who knew that was fashion, back at our school?

A mullet, a mustache—it's hard to believe,
That was considered cool, oh yes, I perceive.
With each laugh, I fondly recall all the quirks,
Like the time on a date, I spilled punch on my shirts!

The cassette tape recorder, oh, what a delight,
We'd sing our own songs, until the late night.
Our voices would crack, our rhythm would wobble,
Yet there in those echoes, we'd still dance and hobble.

Now here we are, wiser, slightly more gray,
With stories that age with each passing day.
But the laughter it lingers, the love still stays near,
In the reflections of past, I hold it all dear.

Whispers of Winter Light

The snowflakes whisper as they fall down slow,
Creating a blanket for all below.
With mugs in our hands and hats on our heads,
We sip cocoa dreams, wrapped up like bread.

The snowman's a sight, with a carrot for plans,
Though he looks a bit more like a group of fans.
His arms made of sticks, a smile so bright,
He waves at the neighbors with frosty delight.

Oh, sledding we go, carving tracks in the snow,
With cries of pure joy and childish hello.
We tumble and tumble, with laughter that sings,
Winter is magic—oh, what joy it brings!

As cold as it gets, in this wintry fright,
We'll dance by the fire, our hearts all alight.
In whispers of warmth, the world turns white,
Together we shine, like stars in the night.

Flickering Shadows of Joy

In the glow of the fire, we laugh and we play,
Telling ghost stories, oh my, what a fray!
With shadows flickering, we jump and we scream,
Are those really ghosts, or just a bad dream?

The popcorn is popping, kernels fly high,
Some land on my lap, oh my, oh my!
With friends gathered close, we munch all the snacks,
Laughter erupts as we dodge those attacks.

A game of charades brings out all the skills,
We impersonate cats, and slam dunk the thrills.
The room is a circus, wild and free,
Delighting in moments, just you and me.

In shadows we dance, with spirits that soar,
Finding the joy in each silly rapport.
As flickering flames join our joyful noise,
We cherish these nights, we embrace the joys.

Radiance Among the Snowflakes

Snowflakes falling, quite the show,
I slipped on one, now off I go.
With arms like flippers, I glide and spin,
Chasing a rabbit, oh what a win!

The snowman grins, he's got my hat,
I grumble loudly, 'Hey! That's not flat!'
But he just chuckles, it's all in fun,
I'll get it back when I'm done with this run!

Winter's chill is quite the tease,
I dream of beaches, and palm tree leaves.
But hey, this snow fort is all the rage,
I'll build a throne and be the snow sage!

Now my nose is red, my toes are cold,
This winter's tale, forever told.
With laughter and snow, we roam the scene,
In this frosty world, we're all quite keen!

Dreams Kindled in the Dark

In the night when shadows creep,
I find my snacks and take a leap.
The cookie jar is my best friend,
With crumbs and chocolate, it'll never end!

Whispers float from the TV glow,
As I dream of places I'd love to go.
But then I stub my toe on a shoe,
Those dreams of grandeur? Oh, boo-hoo!

I drift to lands where floors are soft,
And there's a pizza planet aloft.
I've piloted ships made of cheese so fine,
With pepperoni stars that brightly shine!

Yet morning comes with sunlight's flare,
A rude reminder—I'm not quite there.
But in these dreams, I'll always play,
Until the moon comes back to stay!

Twilight's Embrace of Warmth

The sky's a canvas, hues of pink,
I sip my cocoa, have to think.
A marshmallow whirlpool, oh so grand,
I might just float if life's unplanned!

The evening whispers, "Time for a treat,"
As dinner's aroma drifts down the street.
But starts the chase of the last slice,
I'm on a quest—oh, this will suffice!

Candles flicker, tales are spun,
Of clumsy cats and their daily fun.
"Did you see him jump?" we laugh and snort,
As we recount his last wild sport!

Twilight wraps us, cozy and bright,
With laughter echoing into the night.
So here's to moments where dreams converge,
In twilight's warmth, all vibes emerge!

Hearts Beneath Soft Flickers

Flickering lights like stars that tease,
Under these blankets, oh, I feel at ease.
Popcorn wars in the movie glow,
Bet I can catch one—give it a throw!

The sofa bounces with every cheer,
As the hero's plan begins to veer.
We gasp together, mouths full of snacks,
How many villains can we attack?

It's heart and laughter that fill the room,
When joy bubbles up—as if from a bloom.
With every flicker, a story is passed,
Creating memories that forever last!

So here's to the nights we take our stand,
With silly faces and popcorn in hand.
In hearts beneath soft flickers, we find,
The warmth of friendship, perfectly aligned!

Memories Ignited in the Dark

In the shadows, my socks come alive,
Dancing wildly like they might thrive.
The cat joins in, a furry delight,
Creating chaos throughout the night.

The fridge hums tunes, a midnight choir,
While leftovers leap, fueled by desire.
I stumble, I trip, on toys galore,
Revisiting childhood, oh, what a chore!

Ghosts of snacks past haunt my fears,
As I seek out chips through the tears.
My dreams are filled with pizza and cheese,
Yet, I settle for veggies and peas.

Memories ignite like a spark in the dark,
With laughter and hiccups, it's quite the lark.
So here's to the nights when snacks took the lead,
For in shadows we find the life that we need.

A Symphony of Flickering Lights

In the living room, a lightbulb wanes,
Drooping down like it's got slight pains.
The TV flickers a sitcom refrain,
While I sit and ponder my snack domain.

The lampshade's dancing, I swear it's true,
Becoming a disco ball in my view.
The dog's grooving, tail wagging offbeat,
Even the cat joins, with two left feet.

With each flicker comes a ghostly face,
The remote is missing, a heinous case.
I search for it by the dim light's glance,
Only to find it lost in my pants.

A symphony plays of electric sighs,
As I sit entranced, in light's sweet lies.
Each bulb's a soloist, strumming my heart,
But shushing the silence, it's truly an art.

Embraced by the Warmth of Light

A glow from the lamp that brings me delight,
Filling the room with warmth so bright.
Socks and slippers, a cozy parade,
Wrapped in a blanket, my grand escapade.

Mismatched candles stand, a quirky bunch,
Fencing the shadows as they munch.
The popcorn pops, a fun little game,
As I giggle at all that I claim.

The glow of the fire flickers and spins,
While I sit with comfort—let the fun begin!
A squirrel peeks in, quite the stylish guest,
Trying to raid my food with zest!

In this light, my worries take flight,
Holding hands with the stars so bright.
So here is my toast to the smiles I create,
Embraced by the warmth, it's never too late.

The Cozy Caress of Candles

Candles flicker, a cozy sight,
Whispers of warmth chasing the night.
The wax drips down like a slow parade,
Creating art like a sweet charade.

Scented like cookies, or maybe pie,
I pretend to bake, oh me, oh my!
But all I obtain is a charred stick,
A culinary fail, quick as a flick.

In shadows they cast, I see my fears,
Filling the room with laughter and cheers.
The flame's little dance, a comedic show,
While I munch on snacks and watch the glow.

The cozy caress of flickering light,
Turns bland days into pure delight.
So here's to the candles, my trusty pals,
Keeping the darkness at bay with their spells.

Silent Glow of Winter's Embrace

The snowflakes dance like tiny feet,
They pirouette and can't be beat.
A snowman grins with a carrot nose,
His hat falls off, but nobody knows.

Hot cocoa spills on grandma's lap,
She scolds the kids, then takes a nap.
The dog runs wild, chasing his tail,
While the cat just sits and acts all frail.

Footprints lead to the fridge so bold,
Who sneaked in late? The truth unfolds!
The winter nights, a cozy decree,
We gather round for a cup of tea.

As we laugh and toss the snowball round,
The joy of winter is truly profound.
With every laugh, our hearts do glow,
In winter's arms, we steal the show!

Flickering Whispers in the Frost

The icy wind whispers tales of old,
Of penguins in tuxes and snowmen so bold.
A snowflake lands on uncle's head,
It melts away—just like his bread!

The fireplace crackles, but it's really the cat,
Who jumps around like a bouncing acrobat.
Hot soup's on the stove, but it's gone in a flash,
The kids swoop in for an evening stash.

Lights twinkle like stars on our neighbor's peach,
While he claims they're from outer space; can't wait to teach.
The holiday lights blink in rhythm and rhyme,
A sight to behold at this snowy clime.

So here's to the season of frost and cheer,
With laughter and joy, let's all give a cheer!
In corners, we giggle with friends so dear,
Flickering whispers—winter's best gear!

Hearthside Reflections

Gathered round with a nutty crew,
We spill our secrets as warm fires brew.
Grandpa snores while he thinks he's wise,
A marshmallow's toast leads to silly surprise.

Mom's pie baking, it sings like a song,
But dad tries to help, and it all goes wrong.
Flour on faces and laughter so loud,
Our kitchen resembles a chaotic crowd.

The dog sneaks snacks from the waiting dish,
As we argue who'll win the holiday wish.
The chocolate fudge slowly starts to blend,
And we hope the dessert won't meet its end.

In this cozy corner, we find our delight,
With playful banter stretching late into night.
Hearthside reflections on warmth we embrace,
In our family circle, we've found our place!

Luminance in the Darkened Room

In a room dimly lit, a glow brings cheer,
It's my brother's flashlight—he thinks it's a spear!
A battle of shadows, with giggles on cue,
As he battles the closet, the monsters all "boo!"

The tinsel gets tangled in grandma's hair,
She's a walking Christmas, but does she care?
The lights on the tree blink wildly and tease,
While the cat chases ribbons with cat-like ease.

We gather together, a glow round the way,
With spirits so bright, we can laugh, shout, and play.
The snacks invade the sofa, the crumbs take their claim,
But in this dark room, we're all worth the fame.

So here's to the laughter in rooms dimly lit,
To moments so silly we just can't quit.
With love and smiles, we find our best doom,
In our hearts, it glows bright—like luminance in the room!

Shadows Dance on Snowy Walls

In winter's grip, the shadows prance,
Like penguins caught in a wobbly dance.
They slip and slide, oh what a sight,
As snowflakes giggle with pure delight.

The trees, they shiver, the ground, it creaks,
While squirrels chatter in funny beaks.
Yet here we are, with hot cocoa in hand,
Laughing at shadows, so grand and bland.

A snowman grins with a carrot nose,
But don't you dare step on his toes!
He'll roll his eyes and give you a shove,
As snowflakes shower in a winter love.

With snowy walls, the night is bright,
While shadows dance in their silly flight.
We join the fun, as laughter rings,
In a world where winter joyfully sings.

Warmth Beneath the Starry Sky

Beneath the stars, we sit and chill,
Sharing stories that give us a thrill.
A blanket here, a snack or two,
Under the sky, where dreams come true.

The campfire crackles, it pops and sings,
While roasting marshmallows and other things.
A hotdog flies, oh what a catch,
As laughter erupts, you could hear a scratch!

The stars are blinking, like eyes that tease,
They twinkle and wink, doing as they please.
While we swap tales of monsters and dreams,
And laugh at the ridiculousness of our schemes.

So arm in arm, we gaze at the night,
Warmth fills the air, oh what a delight!
In this little world, with friends so spry,
We find our joy beneath the starry sky.

The Night of Glimmering Hopes

In a town of dreams, where wishes flow,
The night of hopes starts to glow.
Lanterns hanging like shiny hats,
Whispers of joy in conversations chat.

The moon, a giant cheese on high,
Makes us giggle, oh my, oh my!
With fireflies buzzing, like tiny lights,
They zap around like silly sights.

A wish is made on each bright star,
Though some are still parked in their car.
"A penny for thoughts!" a child shouts loud,
As their dreams swirl up, they're feeling proud.

Under the canopy of glimmering dreams,
Hope dances wildly and brightly beams.
So raise your glass, let your spirits soar,
For tonight's the night we all adore!

Candles of Solace and Light

Candles flicker in a cozy nook,
Casting shadows, oh what a look!
They wiggle and dance with a charming flair,
While the cat thinks they're playing fair.

With cozy socks and a cup of tea,
We sit and giggle, just you and me.
A book in hand, or maybe a song,
As candles sing where we belong.

They offer solace, sweet and bright,
While we share stories that feel just right.
But be careful, oh don't let them fight,
For when they argue, it's quite the sight!

So here we gather, hearts feeling light,
With candles glowing through the night.
In this warm haven, we laugh and gleam,
As solace wraps us in a happy dream.

Reflections of Love's Radiance

Love's like a mirror, so shiny and bright,
It shows all your flaws, then says, "You're just right!"
I whisper sweet nothings, she giggles and grins,
Then steps on my toe, and the laughter begins.

Each date's like a circus, both wild and absurd,
With popcorn and laughter, not just a few words.
Romance is a dance, sometimes tripping in style,
But love's in the stumbles, it makes us both smile.

We share all our snacks, while watching a show,
My heart does a flip when she steals my nacho.
Her eyes glimmer bright, just like stars in the sky,
But who knew a kiss could come with a pie?

So here's to our journey, so funny and grand,
With love's little quirks that we both understand.
Through each silly moment, I'll cherish the thrill,
For her laughter's the tune that keeps my heart still.

Glimmers of Faith and Fellowship

Faith's like a candle, it flickers and glows,
In Sunday best shoes, it's where friendship grows.
But let's not forget, we all have our quirks,
Like singing too loud, or doing weird works.

Gathered in church, we share all our dreams,
While passing the peace, it's not as it seems.
A wink and a nod, during hymns that we sing,
And the laughter erupts when we miss a key ring.

Potluck detective, what's under that lid?
Is it casserole magic, or just pizza hid?
We toast to our blessings, and sometimes a pie,
For faith shared with friends can bring tears to the eye.

So here's to our crew, with hearts open wide,
In faith and in laughter, there's nothing to hide.
Through each silly moment, our spirits take flight,
In fellowship's glow, we shine ever bright.

A Lantern for the Soul

A lantern's a beacon, guiding through night,
And sometimes it flickers, like me in a fright.
I trip on the cord while searching for light,
But the laughter I share makes everything right.

With friends by my side, we wander and roam,
Each alleyway's laughter feels just like home.
We crack silly jokes that only we get,
While lighting up paths so we don't lose a bet.

We share our old stories, both silly and sweet,
Of times when we danced with two left feet.
We envy the moon for its glowing crown,
But laugh when it hides and lets stars tumble down.

So let's raise our lanterns, bright souls in a line,
For warmth in our hearts is the true sacred sign.
Together we'll shine, and find joy in the stroll,
With friends as our lanterns, they'll lighten our souls.

Voices Wrapped in Warm Embrace

Voices wrapped in laughter, like a cozy scarf,
We tell our best jokes, oh how they do par!
A hug and a wink, and the giggles arise,
With friends by your side, there's no need for disguise.

In gatherings bright, we share secrets galore,
With eyes all a-twinkle, we're never a bore.
When life feels too heavy, we lighten the load,
Turning frowns into smiles, down this winding road.

Like wind in our hair, we run wild and free,
Our shenanigans echo, just you wait and see.
From funny mishaps to wisdom we share,
In voices wrapped warm, love's always laid bare.

So here's to our crew, the laughter we build,
With hearts all entwined, our joys are fulfilled.
Through each silly moment, let's cherish the grace,
For voices wrapped warm, create the best space.

Glowing Harmony Under Stars

The stars above are shining bright,
While ants below are searching for a bite.
A cat thinks it's a big game of chase,
When really it's just a squirrel's race.

A dog joins in with a joyous bark,
As the moonlight dances in the park.
The owls hoot their comedic tune,
While the mice are plotting under the moon.

Fireflies flicker with a wink and a nudge,
As if they're whispering, 'Do not judge!'
While crickets chirp in rhythm and glee,
It's nighttime chaos, can't you see?

In harmony, they all bump and collide,
This wacky world, where critters abide.
So join the fun, don't be a grouch,
Under the stars, let's all slouch!

The Allure of Soft Shadows

Shadows stretch and begin to yawn,
As sleepy trees wave saying 'Come on!'
The cats lounge low, like they're on a throne,
While the dogs try to fetch a shadowed bone.

A tall tale begins in the dim-lit light,
Of a daring mouse that took on the night.
He tiptoed past boots and old coats piled high,
With a quest for cheese that made him fly.

Lamps flicker on with a soft little sigh,
As the world around starts to simplify.
Chairs creak quietly, as if to share,
Their secrets whispered, light as air.

Oh, the shadows dance like nobody's watching,
Creating a scene that's worth a botching.
With laughter and jokes, they go to and fro,
In this soft-lit world, come on, let's go!

A Celebration in Every Flicker

Each flicker tells a story, it's true,
Of cake crumbs left on the kitchen crew.
The candles burn bright, with the frosting high,
While the kids honk like geese, oh my, oh my!

With paper hats atop their messy heads,
And laughter bubbling like waterbeds.
Pinatas swing, filled with treats galore,
But the blindfolded kid always hits the door.

Balloons float on their colorful rise,
Grabbing at clouds in the nighttime skies.
Party hats wobble, just like the guests,
Trying to dance, but failing their tests.

Yet every flicker is magic for sure,
In laughter and joy, our hearts feel pure.
With each little spark, we know we've struck gold,
In this wonderful night that never gets old!

Embracing the Night's Glow

As twilight wraps the world in embrace,
The stars peek out, keeping up the pace.
With glow-in-the-dark socks, I waddle about,
While the moon giggles, that's what it's about.

Crickets are masters, tuning their band,
Creating a symphony, close at hand.
Toads leap in rhythm, oh what a sight,
In this wild, silly, froggy spotlight.

The glowworms shine like tiny bright lamps,
While fireflies flicker in joyful camps.
The dark can't scare me, I've found my spark,
In the night's embrace, we'll always embark.

So let's dance like shadows, swirl and spin,
Catch the nighttime glow as we dive in.
With laughter and joy in every twirl,
Embracing this night, let the fun unfurl!

Cherished Hours of Reflection

In the mirror, I see a face,
With a snack crumbled all over the place.
Thinking deep thoughts, must solve the riddle,
Of how I lost the remote in the middle.

Time flies, I'm just sitting here,
Gazing at the fridge with a hopeful leer.
Is there cheese? Perhaps a pie?
Oh, look, a sock - how did that get by?

I ponder my life in a comfy chair,
With a cat that gives me a judgmental stare.
Sipping on cocoa, lost in my plight,
Do I want dessert? Well, I just might!

Reflection's a joy when there's treats in sight,
Cherished hours before the midnight bite.
But the cereal calls – I must be strong,
Tomorrow is when the diet goes on!

Echoes of Laughter in the Dark

In the dark, we hear strange sounds,
Like a booted cat that leaps and bounds.
Squeaks and rustles wake the night,
What was that? Just a ghostly fright!

My friend starts telling a spooky tale,
With edits and twists, he's gonna fail.
We laugh so hard, it echoes wide,
Until the neighbor comes to bide.

Under blankets with popcorn and snacks,
Creepy movie? We'll need a few hacks.
Hold my hand if you feel afraid,
Just don't blame me if I need a raid!

The laughter fades, but we're still bold,
Cackling away in the midnight cold.
And when the credits roll and it's done,
We'll tell more stories and just have fun!

The Scent of Pine and Wax

In the woods, the pine trees sway,
With a scent that cheers up the day.
I burned a candle to set the mood,
But now the smoke smells like burnt food!

Wax drips down, oh what a mess,
I tried to clean it, I must confess.
The cat comes by, slips with a shout,
Now he's dancing, what's that about?

The scent of pine wafts through the air,
While candles melt, it's quite the affair.
Not quite a spa day, but it's just fine,
Embrace the chaos, life's a wild line!

So here we are, a blend of two,
Wandering woods with a lovely view.
With candles burning too bright and bold,
The laughter we share is worth more than gold!

Whispered Wishes in the Light

Whispers float like sparkling fireflies,
As I make my wish beneath the skies.
I want a pizza, pepperoni supreme,
But the stars just wink in a nightly dream.

In the sunlight, I sit and scheme,
This wish isn't silly, it's my grand theme!
A cupcake river, chocolate so sweet,
With gummy bears dancing on every street.

I giggle softly; what can go wrong?
My wishes are wild, but I sing this song.
To the moon with a wink and a smile,
Let's make this insanity last for a while!

So here's to wishes, both big and small,
In the light, we wander, we stand tall.
If the world has frosting, let's share a slice,
Whispered wishes make everything nice!

Twilight Dreams Wrapped in Yuletide

In twilight dreams wrapped tight,
Elves in pajamas, what a sight!
Cookies vanish, crumbs remain,
That sneaky Santa, full of gain.

Reindeer games on rooftops loud,
Jingle bells in a silvery shroud.
Hot cocoa spills, oh what a mess!
Sprinkling cheer, we do our best.

Tangled lights we cannot find,
Carolers sing, but they're maligned.
Grandma's snoring like a bear,
While visions of sugar plums fill the air.

With laughter shared all through the night,
Wrapped in warmth, hearts feel so light.
Each moment shifts like snowflakes whirled,
In twilight dreams, our joy unfurled.

The Flicker of Family Gatherings

The flicker of candles on the table,
Uncle Joe tells tales, not quite stable.
Auntie's cooking, a little too hot,
Family love served in a giant pot.

Children darting, they take a peek,
Under the table, the dog plays sneak.
Whispers of secrets hang in the air,
While Grandpa snores without a care.

Leftovers piled, a mountain so grand,
Trying to fit it in one hand.
Laughter erupts like soda pop,
In family gatherings, joy won't stop.

Each little quirk, each silly face,
Makes the chaos feel like grace.
Together we shine, a hilarious crew,
In flickering light, love's the glue.

Glowing Hearts in the Stillness

Amidst the stillness, hearts aglow,
A cat in the tree, oh what a show!
Baking mishaps, flour in the air,
Giggles erupt, there's joy to share.

Soft whispers of stories told,
Grandpa's jokes, a bit too bold.
A toast to fun, we raise our cheer,
With glowing hearts, we hold each dear.

Snowflakes dance, it starts to freeze,
Kids in sleds, zigzag with ease.
Hot cider spills as laughter flows,
In cozy warmth, our bond just grows.

Even if batteries seem to drain,
And that snowman leans like it's in pain,
Together we'll freeze this joyful night,
With glowing hearts, all feels so right.

A Serenade of Flickering Flames

A serenade of flames so bright,
S'more disasters lead to laughter's height.
The marshmallows catch fire, oh dear!
But the tales unfold, bring us near.

Crackling wood and shadows that dance,
While Dad tries to sing, not a chance!
With every crackle, a new memory made,
In flickering light, all worries fade.

Sparks flying like wishes in the sky,
Uncles and aunts, the reasons why,
This chaos of love, in every glance,
Around the fireside, we take our chance.

With stories shared and jokes on repeat,
Our hearts feel warm, our laughter sweet.
In a serenade where love remains,
We gather round, despite the flames.

Whispers in the Warmth of Firelight

The flames do dance, a silly spree,
As marshmallows toast, it's quite a sight!
The shadows play, they laugh with glee,
    In the cozy nook of firelight.

We sing off-key, our voices soar,
The cat just stares, what's all this fuss?
A spark flies out, the dog's on the floor,
I swear it thinks we're all insane—thus!

We tell old tales of ghosts and fright,
But all we see is a weird old broom.
It winks at us in the fading light,
I'm starting to think this house is doomed!

Yet here we sit, with chili and stew,
In comfy chairs that creak and squeak.
With every laugh, our joy renew,
All is bright, though the night is bleak.

Echoes of Joy in Soft Luminescence

In the glow of lamps, we share our dreams,
With popcorn flies across the room.
Beneath the light, the laughter beams,
And spills like sunshine, dispelling gloom.

The cat joins in with a pounce and spin,
As shadows cavort on the walls.
A cornered sock becomes a win,
In this house of giggles and brawls.

We sing to crickets, a tune so grand,
They chirp along, can you hear the tune?
Our voices echo across the land,
As we dance beneath the silvery moon.

With ice cream buckets piled up high,
And sticky fingers all around,
We laugh until we start to cry,
In this blessed light, joy is found.

The Night When Wishes Shine

Beneath the stars, we toss a coin,
In a wishful fountain, a bubbly spree.
"Make me rich!" cries my friend, a join,
While I just wish for more ice tea.

The fireflies flicker, a tiny show,
They wink and nod, in tiny cheer.
"Let's wish for friends!" I blurt, you know,
But some are stuck in the bathroom, dear!

The moonlight smiles, a grand old fellow,
We twirl about, with such delight.
Someone slips, the ground's so yellow,
And soon we're grinning with all our might!

So here's to wishes, both big and small,
To funny moments that make us beam.
With laughter shared, we'll have it all,
In this absurd and lovely dream.

Illuminated Paths to Home

As lanterns swing and lights do twinkle,
We stroll the lanes, our giggles loud.
A squirrel scampers, my friend did crinkle,
Chasing its tail, it's quite proud.

The garden gnomes seem to startle,
With silly hats and grins so wide.
They plot their schemes—how dare they dawdle,
While we just skip with joy in stride!

A wayward cat joins our parade,
It leaps and bounds, it leads the dance.
We're lost in pure, unfiltered play,
Embracing life like a merry chance.

At last, we find our way back home,
With tired feet and hearts aglow.
In every step, we're free to roam,
As laughter echoes, our spirits grow.

The Glow of Togetherness

In a room full of laughter, we all grow,
Sharing socks and secrets, just go with the flow.
A cake's on the counter, half eaten, oh dear!
But friendship's the frosting that brings us good cheer.

When one tells a joke, we all hold our sides,
With snorts and with giggles, oh how fun it slides!
Uncle Fred's in the corner, he's danced 'til he's sore,
We'd tie him down, but he'd still ask for more!

The cat joins our party, a diva supreme,
She knocks down the punch bowl, fulfilling her dream.
Her whiskers all sparkling, she sneers at our plight,
In this glow of togetherness, everything's right!

Let's raise up our glasses, or mugs filled with brew,
To moments so silly, to friendships so true.
In a world that's chaotic, we create our own zone,
The glow isn't just laughter; it's just love on loan!

Children in a Starry Embrace

Under the blanket forts, so cozy and grand,
Tales of brave knights and faraway lands.
With a flashlight as sword, they fight dragons true,
While parents watch closely, with giggles, not boo!

Outside the moon winks, the stars start to dance,
As whispers grow louder, they've taken their chance.
A comet zooms by, and one shouts, "Oh wow!"
Bet they'll remember this moment, somehow!

A snack of rock candy, their space food delight,
They swear it's a meteor that tastes just right.
With sticky pink fingers and grins ear to ear,
In the universe of laughter, there's nothing to fear!

So here in the starlight, dreams sparkle with glee,
They hug tight each other, as happy as can be.
In this magical hour, their worries all fade,
Children in a starry embrace, unafraid!

Luminance in the Cold

Amidst frosty mornings strolled snowmen with flair,
In shades and top hats, they bask without care.
The breath of the icy air billows so white,
As kids throw their snowballs — a glorious sight!

Laughter erupts with each plunge and each slip,
One brave one plops down and lets out a flip.
With cheeks all a-tingle and noses aglow,
We'll conquer this winter, just watch us all go!

The cocoa we sip is rich, sweet as can be,
With marshmallows dancing, oh what joy for me!
But wait! What's this? A snowball fight's started,
As mud pies of laughter leave our plans outsmarted!

We sing silly carols, while tripping through snow,
With mittens that match — or not, as we go.
In this chill, warmth sprouts from the moments we hold,
With luminance shared in this winter so bold!

Twilight's Gentle Embrace

As the sun starts to yawn, it paints skies in gold,
The fireflies flicker, "Hey! Come see us glow!"
With laughter like bubbles that bounce in the air,
Twilight's soft whispers bring peace everywhere.

The swing set is creaky, but still standing strong,
While kids chant sweet melodies, all sing along.
The ice cream truck's ringing, what treats shall we score?

With sticky fingers waving, who could ask for more?

The breeze tells a story, of days full of play,
As dusk gathers gently, we wish it could stay.
With every soft giggle, with every last cheer,
Twilight's gentle embrace wraps us ever near.

So let's twirl and skip 'til the daylight has flown,
In this brief, precious moment, we feel right at home.
As stars peek through curtains, we promise to share,
Twilight's sweet secrets, a memory rare.

A Night Wrapped in Warmth

The blanket's too small for two,
Yet here I am, snuggled with you.
Popcorn's the snack of choice tonight,
We laugh 'til our faces turn bright.

The dog steals my spot with a sigh,
I think he's in on the joke, oh my!
The cat joins in with her regal strut,
Claiming the snack bowl, swatting my gut.

The lights flicker as if in a dance,
Providing the perfect evening romance.
A movie pause for popcorn bliss,
I can't resist a cheeseball kiss!

Outside the snow makes a frosty show,
While inside our banter begins to flow.
With giggles and warmth in every chat,
This cozy night is the best—just like that!

Illumination of Silent Halls

The hallway's quiet, a ghostly sight,
With shadows creeping, oh what a fright!
But then a wink from the bulb above,
Turns my fear to laughter, it's all in love.

I tiptoe softly on creaky floors,
Avoiding the cat who's plotting wars.
A corner turns, and there's a ghost,
Looking quite lost, I wonder who's host!

Behind the curtain, I discover a broom,
Dressed in cobwebs, it runs like a zoom!
A dusty past waits for laughter's call,
In the scary stillness, I stand tall.

Echoes of giggles fill the air,
As I dance around without a care.
Illumination brings joy in spades,
In silent halls, fun never fades!

Hearthside Dreams in Soft Glow

The fire crackles with stories to tell,
While marshmallows roast, oh what a smell!
A recliner calls with a plush embrace,
As laughter echoes in this cozy space.

The dog sprawls out, his dreams take flight,
Chasing squirrels in a sleepy delight.
The cat purrs softly, a snooze in place,
While we share secrets, a warm, happy face.

Our mugs are full with cocoa divine,
Sip slowly, savoring each little line.
Between every laugh and silly joke,
The flames dance wildly, like friendly smoke.

With hearts aglow and dreams that weave,
In hearthside warmth, we dare to believe.
This soft glow of night, with family near,
Turns ordinary moments into sheer cheer.

The Gentle Flicker of Tradition

Each year we gather round the old tree,
Tangled lights, where did they flee?
Ornaments clash with stories untold,
Tradition's a mess, yet it never gets old.

Aunts bring cookies, a sweet, sweet mess,
Cousins compete in a gingerbread fest.
Who can build the tallest, they shout and cheer,
While icing drips and we laugh—oh dear!

Dad finds the tinsel, what a tangle,
His concentration makes us mangle.
"Just one more!" he insists, and we giggle,
As he unties knots while we all wiggle.

As candles flicker, hearts full of glee,
We reminisce about the wild old spree.
Traditions bind us, weird and sweet,
In this gentle flicker, we feel complete.

Illuminated Secrets of the Heart

There once was a fellow named Clyde,
Who tripped on a shoelace and cried.
His heart was so bright,
It lit up the night!

Illuminated Secrets of the Heart

His secrets were stored in a jar,
Right next to his old rusty car.
He'd open it fast,
But it burst like a blast!

Illuminated Secrets of the Heart

With cookies and candies galore,
He couldn't resist, he'd ignore.
He ate all the treats,
And danced on his feet!

Illuminated Secrets of the Heart

Now Clyde is a legend, they say,
 For spilling his candy one day.
  His heart like a kid,
   In laughter, he hid!

Illuminated Secrets of the Heart

With secrets as sweet as his smiles,
He lights up our lives with his wiles.
So here's to the man,
With a heart made of sand!

A Tapestry of Light and Shadow

I met a horse named Barry Bright,
Who painted the world with delight.
His mane was a mix,
Of polka dots and bricks!

A Tapestry of Light and Shadow

He danced across fields with great flair,
While butterflies sparked in the air.
His hooves tapped a beat,
That made all hearts greet!

A Tapestry of Light and Shadow

But one fateful day, oh dear me,
Barry tripped on his own cup of tea.
He spilled it all wide,
And slipped with great pride!

A Tapestry of Light and Shadow

With laughter, we rolled on the grass,
As Barry just looked for a pass.
His charm's hard to beat,
In his muddy retreat!

A Tapestry of Light and Shadow

So if you find Barry around,
Remember to treasure this sound.
For laughter's the key,
To light hearts with glee!

Embered Nights and Sweet Memories

On embered nights, we sat by the fire,
With marshmallows to roast, we conspired.
But sticky and gooey,
My fingers got chewy!

Embered Nights and Sweet Memories

We told silly stories and laughed,
While s'mores turned our jaws into craft.
A chocolatey cheer,
Was all we held dear!

Embered Nights and Sweet Memories

But then came a loud, sudden crack,
A squirrel darted in for a snack.
As chaos erupted,
Our snacks all corrupted!

Embered Nights and Sweet Memories

We chased after him, running with glee,
Trying to catch up, oh dear me!
Yet in the end,
Our laughter would blend!

Embered Nights and Sweet Memories

So here's to those nights filled with cheer,
With friends close by, always near.
In memories bright,
Your heart takes its flight!

The Dance of Flame and Spirit

In the moonlight, we danced like flames,
With quirky old tunes and strange names.
Our feet rhythmically thumped,
While my hat fell, it clumped!

The Dance of Flame and Spirit

My friend brought a hat full of chips,
He wore it with pride on his lips.
But in the first spin,
A chip flew right in!

The Dance of Flame and Spirit

Our giggles lit up the night sky,
Like fireworks bursting up high.
With laughter so bright,
We danced till the light!

The Dance of Flame and Spirit

So when the world gets too serious,
Remember to dance, be delirious!
With flames that ignite,
Let spirits take flight!

Flickering Stories of Old

Once a lamp told tales so bright,
Of cats in capes and birds in flight.
But when the battery said goodnight,
The stories flickered, lost to sight.

A squirrel once flew on a broom,
Chasing its nuts to outer space doom.
It landed hard, with quite the boom,
Now it just lives in the attic's gloom.

The ghost of a sock, quite unwound,
Haunts the dryer, twirling round and round.
It claims it's the best dancer in town,
But only spins when the humans are found.

So gather 'round for tales so silly,
Of dancing bread and flying willy-nilly.
Old stories may sound a bit frilly,
But they miss the fun, oh, dear, how silly!

The Canvas of Night's Warm Hues

The moon wore pajamas, snug and tight,
Painting the stars in colors so bright.
It painted clouds with a splash of delight,
While crickets chirped, and the owl said, "Alright!"

A raccoon with shades walks down the street,
In search of some snacks, oh, what a treat!
He steals a doughnut, oh what a feat,
And dances away on his tiny, cute feet.

The night whispered secrets through trees that swayed,
While fireflies glimmered in the dusk that played.
A cat took a nap in the shade it laid,
And dreamed of fish, as the stars displayed.

So paint your dreams with colors so bright,
Let laughter reign through this splendid night.
For in every shadow, there shines a light,
As we dance with the stars, everything feels right!

Hearts alight with Wonder

In a jar of jelly, a jellybean sighed,
"Why can't I roll?" it awkwardly cried.
The gumballs giggled, all piled aside,
As rainbow sprinkles danced, bursting with pride.

The fridge had a party, foods in a trance,
With pickles doing the salsa, oh what a dance!
The leftovers joined in, taking a chance,
Brought out their old tunes, made us all prance.

A cupcake with frosting, all fluffy and sweet,
Wobbled and jiggled on its two little feet.
It shouted, "Let's party, let's all have a seat!"
And donuts all cheered, what a tasty treat!

So here's to the wonder that never grows old,
From jellybeans dancing to stories retold.
In hearts alight, let us all be bold,
For laughter and joy are treasures to hold!

A Minuet of Lighted Dreams

The stars began to twirl and sway,
In a minuet, they danced away.
While whispering wishes, like kids at play,
They chuckled in sparkle, oh what a display!

The moon was the DJ, spinning with flair,
While comets did the cha-cha, zooming in air.
A nightingale crooned, not a single care,
As twinkling lights shimmered everywhere.

The shadows in corners started to groove,
With chairs doing backflips, oh what a move!
The dreams all gathered, ready to prove,
That even in night's quiet, spirits can soothe.

So close your eyes and join the dance,
In a world where dreams take a chance.
For in this minuet, let laughter enhance,
As we sway in the glow, lost in a trance!

Solitary Glimmers of Peace

In a quiet room with a cat,
I ponder life while he takes a nap.
He dreams of mice, I dream of cake,
No noise or fuss, just a peaceful break.

The phone's left off, the door's locked tight,
Moments of calm, oh what a delight.
I sip my tea, it's chamomile sweet,
While the cat snores softly, it can't be beat.

Outside does thrum with its busy craze,
Cars honk and people shout in a maze.
Yet here I dwell in this soft, warm glow,
With my furry friend, we just take it slow.

So here's my toast to those quiet times,
When the worst of the world doesn't cost a dime.
Just me and my thoughts, and the cat on my knee,
In solitary glimmers, I find my glee.

Flickers of Love Amongst the Pines

Beneath the pines where we would roam,
You wore that hat that made me moan.
"Why wear that thing?" I teased with delight,
"Because it's cozy!" you said, holding tight.

We danced like fools, lost in the trees,
You caught your foot and fell with a sneeze.
A flicker of laughter, the sound of a snort,
In love, my dear, we both fall short.

Your heart is gentle, like a soft breeze,
But your dance moves could cause some unease.
Yet in this chaos, all's perfectly fine,
Flickers of love beneath the pine.

So let's wander again, hand in hand,
Amidst the needles, let laughter stand.
With every slip, with every near miss,
In these flickers of love, there's simple bliss.

A Tapestry of Light and Memory

In grandma's attic, where dust bunnies dwell,
I stumbled upon a strange, glowing shell.
It whispered tales of days gone by,
Of pie fights and dreams that danced in the sky.

There's Uncle Fred in a polka-dot suit,
Holding a cake that looks just like a boot.
A tapestry woven of laughter and joy,
What's a simple family without some annoy?

The lights of the past flicker wild and bright,
Like a disco ball at a Saturday night.
We reminisce while we're giggling loud,
In this quirky patchwork, we're always proud.

So let's fill our hearts with these colorful views,
With memories stitched in a carnival of hues.
For every laugh, and each silly cheer,
Forms a tapestry filled with love, never fear.

Winter's Gentle Embrace in Glow

Oh winter's come with its frosty bite,
Yet in our home, everything feels just right.
With cocoa in hand and a blanket to share,
We snuggle together, without a care.

The snowflakes fall like feathers from heaven,
But outside, my neighbor's looped around eleven.
I watch him slip on ice with a yelp,
Winter's grip has him, and I can't help a help.

We build up a snowman with a carrot for a nose,
Decorated with gumdrops in neat little rows.
He grins as he stands, as proud as can be,
Until the dog comes, and "crunch!" says he!

So here's to winter, and its chilly embrace,
Where laughter lingers in every cold space.
As we bundle up tight, in all this white glow,
We find joy in the warmth, through the frost and the snow.

Milton Keynes UK
Ingram Content Group UK Ltd.
UKHW010228111224
452348UK00011B/582